KING CRABS

Bethany Baxter

PowerKiDS press™

New York

For my friends at Belmar Elementary School

Published in 2014 by The Rosen Publishing Group, Inc.
29 East 21st Street, New York, NY 10010

First Edition

Editor: Julia Quinlan
Book Design: Greg Tucker

Photo Credits: Cover Gustav Verderber/Visuals Unlimited/Getty Images; p. 4 Rondi Church/Photo Researchers/ Getty Images; p. 5 Amanda Nicholls/Shutterstock.com; p. 6 Cyril Hou/Shutterstock.com; p. 7 Ira Block/National Geographic/Getty Images; p. 8 © iStockphoto.com/lightasafeather; p. 9 Papa1266/Shutterstock.com; pp. 10, 14, 15, 17 Robert F. Sisson/National Geographic/Getty Images; p. 11 © imagebroker.net/Superstock; © pp. 12–13 Visual & Written/Superstock; p. 16 electerra/Shutterstock.com; p. 18 Thomas Kitchin & Victoria Hurst/First Light/Getty Images; p. 19 Boris Pamikov/Shutterstock.com; p. 20 Jean-Erick Pasquier/Gammo-Rapho/Getty Images; p. 21 Wyatt Rivard/ Shutterstock.com; p. 22 Michael Melford/National Geographic/Getty Images.

Library of Congress Cataloging-in-Publication Data

Baxter, Bethany.
 King crabs / by Bethany Baxter. — First edition.
     pages cm. — (Awesome armored animals)
 Includes index.
 ISBN 978-1-4777-0793-7 (library binding) — ISBN 978-1-4777-0958-0 (pbk.) —
 ISBN 978-1-4777-0959-7 (6-pack)
 1. King crabs—Juvenile literature. I. Title.
 QL444.M33B386 2014
 595.3'87—dc23

                               2012045532

Manufactured in the United States of America

CPSIA Compliance Information: Batch #S13PK6: For Further Information contact Rosen Publishing, New York, New York at 1-800-237-9932

Contents

Armored Kings 4

Coldwater Homes 6

Five Pairs of Legs 8

Molting and Migrating 10

Cool Crab Facts! 12

Eggs, Larvae, and Pods 14

What Do Crabs Eat? 16

King Crab Predators 18

Fishing for Crabs 20

Keeping Crabs Safe 22

Glossary 23

Index 24

Websites 24

Armored Kings

King crabs are animals that live on the ocean floor. Their bodies are covered in tough shells that act as body armor. Their shells are so hard that few ocean **predators** can break them.

There are about 40 **species** of king crabs. King crabs are often named for the color or shape of their shell.

This red king crab was found in Alaska. Its hard shell keeps it safe from many predators.

Lobsters are related to king crabs. They are both crustaceans. Lobsters have claws and hard shells, as king crabs do.

For example, red king crabs have a dark red shell, while blue king crabs are bluish. Spiny king crabs are covered in long, sharp spines.

King crabs are crustaceans with ten legs. Crustaceans are a group of hard-shelled ocean animals. Other crustaceans include lobsters, shrimp, and prawns.

Coldwater Homes

King crabs are found in Earth's cold northern oceans. In the United States, most king crabs live in the North Pacific Ocean around Alaska. However, some can be found as far south as California. Many king crabs are also found off the coast of Siberia, in Russia, and in the waters around Japan.

Adult king crabs live on the ocean floor. However, some king crabs live in deeper waters than others.

King crabs such as this one, live deep underwater, on the ocean floor.

Blue king crabs live in the icy waters around the Diomede Islands, which are between Alaska and Siberia in the Bering Strait.

Blue king crabs generally live in waters less than 650 feet (198.1 m) deep, while red king crabs may live in waters 800 feet (244 m) deep. Golden king crabs can be found in waters as deep as 1,800 feet (549 m)!

Five Pairs of Legs

King crabs do not have skeletons inside their bodies. Their hard shells are **exoskeletons**. Their legs are covered by the exoskeleton, too. All king crabs have five pairs of legs. The first pair is the crabs' claws. The middle three pairs are used for walking. The last pair of legs are very small and used only for **mating**. King crabs also have fan-shaped tails. These stay folded under their bodies.

This king crab might look big, but they can grow even larger!

The two small legs used for mating are tucked under the king crab's carapace. The carapace is a piece of shell that covers the back of the king crab.

Red king crabs are the largest king crabs. Males can weigh up to 24 pounds (11 kg). Their legs can span 5 feet (1.5 m) across.

King crab shells do not get bigger as the crab grows. Instead, king crabs shed, or **molt**, their old shells and make new ones. When a crab is ready to molt, it absorbs a lot of water and swells. Then, it pops open its old shell and backs out wearing a new shell. The new shell takes days to harden. King crabs may molt between 15 and 20 times during their lives.

These young king crabs are traveling in a pod, or group of crabs, for protection. It is safer for them to walk together than alone.

These king crabs are moving along the seafloor together.

In the late winter, adult king crabs **migrate** from deep water to shallow water near the shore. There, they mate and molt. Then, in the spring, they migrate back to deep waters to find food.

Cool Crab Facts!

1. King crab shells are made mostly of calcium. Calcium is a hard substance also found in human bones and teeth.

2. King crabs' two front claws are not the same size. The right claw is much bigger than the left. They use this claw for crushing food.

3. Golden king crabs are much smaller than red or blue king crabs. However, they have the largest eggs of any king crabs.

4. It is easy to tell male and female red king crabs apart, even if they are the same size. This is because males have a triangle-shaped tail, while females' tails are more rounded.

5. Female king crabs make tens of thousands of eggs when they mate. For example, a female red king crab can make between 50,000 and 500,000 eggs a year.

6. King crabs' legs fold backward, unlike the forward-folding legs of other kinds of crabs. This means that they can walk straight forward. Most other crabs can only walk sideways.

7. Blue king crabs mate only once every two years, unlike red king crabs who mate every year.

8. Scientists think red and blue king crabs can live up to 30 years in the wild.

Male and female king crabs mate in shallow waters. After mating, the female crab carries the eggs under her tail for about a year. **Larvae** hatch from the eggs in the spring.

Larvae first look like very small shrimp. They float in the ocean water and feed on tiny plants and animals for a few months. After molting several times, they change into small crabs that settle on the ocean floor.

Young king crabs must molt many times before they reach full size. This juvenile king crab is backing out of its old shell.

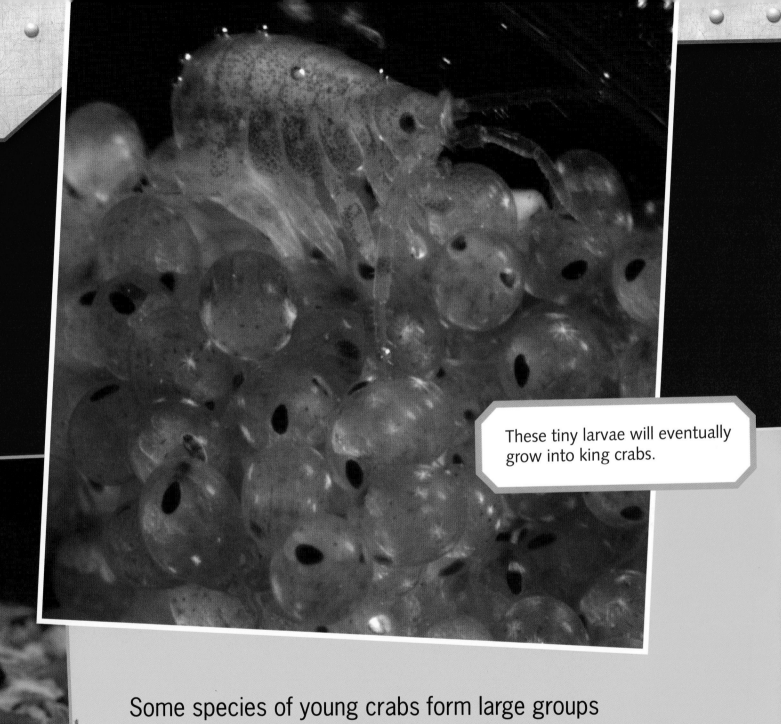

These tiny larvae will eventually grow into king crabs.

Some species of young crabs form large groups called pods. Pods stay together in shallow waters to grow, molt, and feed until the crabs reach adult size.

Adult king crabs eat whatever they can find on the ocean floor. For smaller crabs, this includes algae, worms, clams, and other small ocean plants and animals. Larger crabs eat live mussels, barnacles, fish, sea stars, sea urchins, and sand dollars, among other animals. They may also eat pieces of dead animals that drift to the ocean floor.

Mussels are a favorite meal of king crabs. There are small animals living inside of the shells.

King crabs are not picky eaters. This brittle star is about to be a meal for this king crab.

King crabs have a strong sense of smell. This helps them find food to eat. They reach out and grasp their food with their claws. Then they use their claws to crush and tear it apart before moving it to their mouths.

King Crab Predators

Many ocean animals eat small king crabs. Fish such as Pacific cod, yellow sole, and halibut are king crab predators. Other predators include octopuses, sea otters, and other crabs. King crabs sometimes eat other king crabs. There are also species of sea worms that eat king crab larvae.

Sea otters are furry mammals that live on the coast of the Pacific Northwest of the United States. They eat many different sea animals, including king crabs.

Octopuses, like this one, will make a meal of king crabs.

However, large king crabs do not have many predators. They are kept safe from most predators by their strong, spiny shells. The only time these crabs are **vulnerable** is right after they have molted. This is because their new shells are still soft for a time after molting.

Fishing for Crabs

In Alaska, blue, red, and golden king crabs are caught and then sold all over the world. These crabs have rich, sweet meat that people enjoy eating. However, there is a very short season during which people are allowed to catch king crabs each year. This is because red and blue crab **populations** have been getting smaller. It is important to keep the crabs safe from **overfishing** so that they do not die out.

This Alaskan fisherman is pulling a pot of king crabs out of the Bering Sea. The crabs will be sorted and sold.

Fishermen take big boats out into the sea to catch king crabs. This boat is headed out into the Bering Sea.

Only male king crabs can be caught and sold in Alaska. This is because female crabs carry eggs. If they are caught, their eggs will not have a chance to hatch and fewer crabs will be born.

Keeping Crabs Safe

The United States has laws that keep king crabs safe from overfishing. However, in other parts of the world, king crabs are caught all year long. **Climate change** and **pollution** also hurt king crab habitats. King crab populations could be in danger because of this.

King crabs' tough armor can protect them from many threats. But, it cannot protect them from such serious threats as climate change, pollution, and overfishing. Luckily there are **conservation** groups working to keep king crabs and other ocean animals from dying out.

Many people like to eat king crabs, but it is important to conserve them as well. King crabs are important to their environments.

Glossary

climate change (KLY-mut CHAYNJ) Changes in Earth's weather that are caused by things people do.

conservation (kon-sur-VAY-shun) Protecting something from harm.

exoskeletons (ek-soh-SKEH-leh-tunz) Hard coverings on the outside of animals' bodies that hold, and guard, the soft insides.

larvae (LAHR-vee) Insects or other animals in the early life stage in which they have a wormlike form.

mating (MAYT-ing) Joining together to make babies.

migrate (MY-grayt) To move from one place to another.

molt (MOHLT) To shed hair, feathers, shell, horns, or skin.

overfishing (oh-ver-FISH-ing) Catching too many fish.

pollution (puh-LOO-shun) Man-made wastes that harm Earth's air, land, or water.

populations (pop-yoo-LAY-shunz) Groups of animals or people living in the same area.

predators (PREH-duh-terz) Animals that kill other animals for food.

species (SPEE-sheez) A single kind of living thing. All people are one species.

vulnerable (VUL-neh-ruh-bel) Open to attack or harm.

Index

A
Alaska, 6, 20–21
armor, 4, 22

C
calcium, 12
California, 6
claw(s), 8, 12, 17
climate change, 22
conservation, 22
crustaceans, 5

E
eggs, 12–14, 21
exoskeleton(s), 8

F
fish, 16, 18
floor, 4, 6, 14, 16
food, 11–12, 17

H
habitats, 22

L
larvae, 14, 18
legs, 5, 8–9, 13
lobsters, 5

M
meat, 20
migrate, 11
molt, 10–11, 15

O
ocean(s), 4–6, 14, 16,
    18, 22
overfishing, 20, 22

P
plants, 14, 16

pods, 15
pollution, 22
populations, 20, 22
prawns, 5
predators, 4, 18–19

S
season, 20
shell(s), 4–5, 8, 10, 12, 19
shrimp, 5, 14
skeletons, 8
species, 4, 15, 18
spines, 5
spring, 11, 14

T
tail(s), 8, 12, 14

W
winter, 11

Websites

Due to the changing nature of Internet links, PowerKids Press has developed an online list of websites related to the subject of this book. This site is updated regularly. Please use this link to access the list: www.powerkidslinks.com/aaa/kcrab/